Health Wellness & Selfcare Journal

Personal Information

Name: ______________________________

Address: ______________________________

City/State/Zip: ______________________________

Phone: ______________________________

Cell: ______________________________

Email: ______________________________

Church: ______________________________

"For I know the plans I have for you," declares the LORD, "plans to prosper you and not to harm you, plans to give you hope and a future."

Jeremiah 29:11

God is able to do exceedingly abundantly above all that we ask or think,
according to the power that works in us.
Ephesians 3:20

Psalm 103: 1-5

Bless the Lord, O my soul: and all that is within me,
bless his holy name.
Bless the Lord, O my soul, and forget not all his benefits:

Who forgives all my sins; who heals all my diseases;
Who redeems my life from destruction;
who crowns me with
lovingkindness and tender mercies;

Who satisfies my mouth with good things;
so that my youth is renewed
like the eagle's.

Ideas For Selfcare

- Start a journal to record your thoughts and experiences.
- Take a mental health day, and do not feel an ounce of guilt about it
- Unplug for an hour. Switch everything to airplane mode and free yourself from the constant bings of social media and email.
- Write encouraging affirmations or inspirational quotes on Post-its and place them where you will see them every day.
- Start a compliments file. Document the great things people say about you, to read later
- Scream, pound pillows, tear up paper, or shake your body to move the energy out.
- Burn a candle or diffuse some oils that have scents that bring you joy
- Walk around the grocery store without a list; Buy some stuff just for fun
- Go hiking, camping, or backpacking and spend some time in nature.
- Sing at the top of your lungs, in the car, with the windows down
- Go to the library or bookstore; Sit in a comfy chair and read
- Go cloud-watching. Lie on your back, relax, and watch the clouds float by
- Do something crafty: knitting, sewing, painting...
- Take a bubble bath with candles and calming music
- Attend a church or spiritual community service.
- Sit in a coffee shop and sip on a luxurious drink
- Listen to a chapter or two from an audiobook.
- Sit on the front porch; Just sit and do nothing
- Go out and spend 10 minutes under the sun.
- Have a dance party to your favorite music
- Go for a drive - no destination required
- Pick or buy a bouquet of fresh flowers
- Do some quick, deep breathing exercises.
- Wrap yourself in a soft, warm blanket
- Give yourself a pedicure or a manicure
- Read a book or magazine for an hour
- Take a leisurely walk without a goal
- Eat your favorite comfort food.
- Put on a homemade face mask
- Watch funny YouTube videos
- Color in your coloring book
- Work on a jigsaw puzzle
- Try out a new hobby
- Look at the stars
- Meditate or pray
- Sit in the sun
- Take a nap

40

Healthy Habits For A Better Life

- Keep a food journal
- Drink at least 8 ounces of fluids everyday
- Eat plenty of fruits and vegetables
- Avoid processed food
- Follow a weekly meal plan
- Quit smoking
- Avoid alcohol
- Cut back on sugar
- Eat whole foods as much as possible
- Go for a walk
- Ride a bike
- Ditch the elevator for the stairs
- Don't snack if you're not hungry
- Don't overeat
- Use a smaller plate
- Maintain a healthy body weight
- Stretch daily to increase flexibility
- When cooking: boil, steam or bake, rather than frying
- Enjoy the great outdoors
- Try prayer and meditation
- Go to bed earlier
- Take up gardening
- Wear clothes that make you happy
- Think positively
- Do not judge yourself
- Read a chapter of a good book everyday
- Don't compare yourself to others
- Throw away things that you do not need
- Enjoy the simple things in life
- Keep pushing forward - Do not give-up
- Pay attention to your feelings
- Laugh often
- Take time to rest
- Surround yourself with positive people
- Listen to inspirational music
- Focus on your blessings
- Practice gratitude
- Value your alone time
- Do a daily, "thought-dump"
- Don't worry

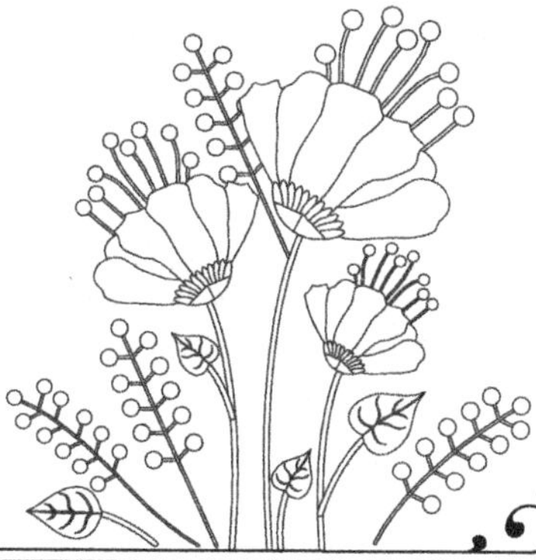

Whether I eat or drink or whatever I do, I will do it all for the glory of God. (1 Corinthians 10:31)

7 Steps To A Healthier Lifestyle

Keep A Food Journal - When you are trying to eat healthier, keeping a food journal can help to promote better nutrition, manage portion size, identify unhealthy habits that are stopping you from losing weight, and help you to make positive lifestyle changes. Writing down every snack, sip of soda, or carb that you consume will make you more accountable for what you are eating.

Watch Your Weight - Being overweight can increase the risk of certain cancers (breast, colon, endometrial), heart disease, type 2 diabetes. Dropping just 5% of your body weight can substantially lower the risk of these diseases. There are some simple things that you can do to control your weight e.g. reduce portion size, sleep more and stress less, use intermittent fasting, eat more whole foods and less processed junk foods, fill up on veggies, drink plenty of water, be active.

Make Smart Food Choices - Making plant food choices such as: produce, legumes, nuts, and whole grains, or low-fat dairy, and small amounts of healthy fat, such as olive can help to prevent serious health problems. People who follow a 70% plant-based diet had a 20 percent lower risk of dying from a heart attack or stroke than those whose diets centered around meat and dairy.

Get Fit - Physical activity helps keep your heart and lungs working efficiently, reduces illness, and ease pain. Ideally it is important to get at least 5 hours of moderate activity each week. e.g. brisk walking, cycling, swimming, or 2.5 hours of vigorous movement, such as jogging, along with resistance training such as lifting light weights. However, moving frequently throughout the day can be very beneficial to your overall health and wellbeing, as well. If you usually sit for long stretches of time, try to take short "activity breaks". Research shows that moving around (or simply standing up) for a few minutes every hour helps bring blood sugar, for instance, closer to normal.

Get Plenty Of Sleep - When you are sleep-deprived, your body secretes high amounts of the hormones cortisol and insulin, both of which increases the risk of heart disease. Getting 7 to 8 hours of sleep each night has several benefits. It can help you to retain your memory, manage your hunger levels, and maintain your immune system (reducing the likelihood of falls, car accidents and illnesses such as coronary artery disease and type 2 diabetes) .

Quit Bad Habits - If you smoke, try to quit, even e-cigs can have long term effects on your health. Smoking can harm your heart and respiratory system. It is also linked to a higher risk of age-related macular degeneration and cataracts. Studies have shown that over 30% of cancer deaths can be attributed to tobacco. Drink moderately, or not at all, people who have less than a drink per week actually live the longest. Try to limit yourself to two drinks per day for men and one for women.

Love Yourself And Be Happy - Self-care affects your physical, mental, emotional and spiritual health. It gives you a break from the everyday stresses of life and time alone to focus on your own well-being. It's difficult to avoid stress altogether, but coping strategies such as deep, slow breathing, aerobic exercise, prayer and meditation, massage, music, reading, gardening and other hobbies can help you manage tension and reduce associated health risks.

I discipline my body and keep it under control, so that after preaching to others, I myself will not be disqualified. (1 Corinthians 9:27)

DAY 28	SU MO TU WE TH FR SA DATE: ______________	How Do I Feel Today ☐ ☐ ☐ ☐
BREAKFAST	LUNCH	DINNER

SNACKS:

TOTAL CALORIES	GLASSES OF WATER	HOURS OF SLEEP

WEIGHT	BLOOD PRESSURE	BLOOD SUGAR

EXERCISE/ PHYSICAL ACTIVITY	SELF-CARE ACTIVITY

I will love the Lord my God with all my heart and with all my soul and with all my mind.
(Matthew 22:37)

DAY 29	SU MO TU WE TH FR SA DATE: ____________	How Do I Feel Today ☐ ☐ ☐ ☐

BREAKFAST	LUNCH	DINNER

SNACKS:

TOTAL CALORIES	GLASSES OF WATER	HOURS OF SLEEP

WEIGHT	BLOOD PRESSURE	BLOOD SUGAR

EXERCISE/ PHYSICAL ACTIVITY	SELF-CARE ACTIVITY

Whatever is true, whatever is honorable, whatever is just, whatever is pure, whatever is lovely, whatever is commendable, if there is any excellence, if there is anything worthy of praise, I will focus on those things.
(Philippians 4:8)

DAY 30	SU MO TU WE TH FR SA DATE: ______________	How Do I Feel Today ☐ ☐ ☐ ☐
BREAKFAST	LUNCH	DINNER

SNACKS:

TOTAL CALORIES	GLASSES OF WATER	HOURS OF SLEEP

WEIGHT	BLOOD PRESSURE	BLOOD SUGAR

EXERCISE/ PHYSICAL ACTIVITY	SELF-CARE ACTIVITY

I will seek the Lord, when I feel weary and burdened, and He will give me rest.
(Matthew 11:28)

DAY 31	SU MO TU WE TH FR SA DATE: ______________	How Do I Feel Today ☐ ☐ ☐ ☐
BREAKFAST	LUNCH	DINNER

SNACKS:

TOTAL CALORIES	GLASSES OF WATER	HOURS OF SLEEP

WEIGHT	BLOOD PRESSURE	BLOOD SUGAR

EXERCISE/ PHYSICAL ACTIVITY	SELF-CARE ACTIVITY

I will trust in the Lord with my whole heart and never rely on what I think I know.
(Proverbs 3:5)

DAY 32

SU MO TU WE TH FR SA

DATE: ____________________

How Do I Feel Today

☐ ☐ ☐ ☐

BREAKFAST

LUNCH

DINNER

SNACKS:

TOTAL CALORIES

GLASSES OF WATER

HOURS OF SLEEP

WEIGHT

BLOOD PRESSURE

BLOOD SUGAR

EXERCISE/ PHYSICAL ACTIVITY

SELF-CARE ACTIVITY

I will always allow the Lord to lead me, and he will show me the right path to take.
(Proverbs 3:6)

DAY 33	SU MO TU WE TH FR SA DATE: ______________	How Do I Feel Today

BREAKFAST	LUNCH	DINNER

SNACKS:

TOTAL CALORIES	GLASSES OF WATER	HOURS OF SLEEP

WEIGHT	BLOOD PRESSURE	BLOOD SUGAR

EXERCISE/ PHYSICAL ACTIVITY	SELF-CARE ACTIVITY

You are my hiding place, oh Lord; you will protect me from trouble and surround me with songs of deliverance. (Psalm 32:7-8)

DAY 34

SU MO TU WE TH FR SA

DATE: ____________________

How Do I Feel Today

BREAKFAST	LUNCH	DINNER

SNACKS:

TOTAL CALORIES	GLASSES OF WATER	HOURS OF SLEEP

WEIGHT	BLOOD PRESSURE	BLOOD SUGAR

EXERCISE/ PHYSICAL ACTIVITY	SELF-CARE ACTIVITY

I am chosen and loved by God. (*Colossians* 3:12)

DAY 35	SU MO TU WE TH FR SA DATE: ______________	How Do I Feel Today ☐ ☐ ☐ ☐
BREAKFAST	LUNCH	DINNER
SNACKS:		
TOTAL CALORIES	GLASSES OF WATER	HOURS OF SLEEP
WEIGHT	BLOOD PRESSURE	BLOOD SUGAR
EXERCISE/ PHYSICAL ACTIVITY	SELF-CARE ACTIVITY	

My God will supply all of my needs according to his riches in glory, in Christ Jesus.
(Philippians 4:19)

DAY 36

SU MO TU WE TH FR SA

DATE: ______________

How Do I Feel Today

☐ ☐ ☐ ☐

BREAKFAST	LUNCH	DINNER

SNACKS:

TOTAL CALORIES	GLASSES OF WATER	HOURS OF SLEEP

WEIGHT	BLOOD PRESSURE	BLOOD SUGAR

EXERCISE/ PHYSICAL ACTIVITY	SELF-CARE ACTIVITY

I will have complete boldness, so that now as always, Christ will be honored in my body.
(Philippians 1:20)

DAY 37

SU MO TU WE TH FR SA

DATE: ______________

How Do I Feel Today

☐ ☐ ☐ ☐

BREAKFAST	LUNCH	DINNER

SNACKS:

TOTAL CALORIES	GLASSES OF WATER	HOURS OF SLEEP

WEIGHT	BLOOD PRESSURE	BLOOD SUGAR

EXERCISE/ PHYSICAL ACTIVITY	SELF-CARE ACTIVITY

For no one ever hated his own flesh, but nourishes and cherishes it, just as Christ does the church, because I am a member of his body. (Ephesians 5:29-30)

DAY 38	SU MO TU WE TH FR SA DATE: ________________	How Do I Feel Today ☐ ☐ ☐ ☐
BREAKFAST	LUNCH	DINNER

SNACKS:

TOTAL CALORIES	GLASSES OF WATER	HOURS OF SLEEP

WEIGHT	BLOOD PRESSURE	BLOOD SUGAR

EXERCISE/ PHYSICAL ACTIVITY	SELF-CARE ACTIVITY

The eye is the lamp of the body. So, if my eye is healthy, my whole body will be full of light
(Matthew 6:22)

DAY 39

SU MO TU WE TH FR SA

DATE: ____________________

How Do I Feel Today

☐ ☐ ☐ ☐

BREAKFAST	LUNCH	DINNER

SNACKS:

TOTAL CALORIES	GLASSES OF WATER	HOURS OF SLEEP

WEIGHT	BLOOD PRESSURE	BLOOD SUGAR

EXERCISE/ PHYSICAL ACTIVITY	SELF-CARE ACTIVITY

It is not for kings to drink wine, or for rulers to take strong drink, lest they drink and forget what has been decreed and pervert the rights of all the afflicted. (Proverbs 31:4-5)

DAY 40

SU MO TU WE TH FR SA

DATE: ____________________

How Do I Feel Today

☐ ☐ ☐ ☐

BREAKFAST	LUNCH	DINNER

SNACKS:

TOTAL CALORIES	GLASSES OF WATER	HOURS OF SLEEP

WEIGHT	BLOOD PRESSURE	BLOOD SUGAR

EXERCISE/ PHYSICAL ACTIVITY	SELF-CARE ACTIVITY

For you formed my inward parts, oh Lord; you knitted me together in my mother's womb.
(Psalm 139:13)

DAY 41

SU MO TU WE TH FR SA

DATE: ____________________

How Do I Feel Today

BREAKFAST	LUNCH	DINNER

SNACKS:

TOTAL CALORIES	GLASSES OF WATER	HOURS OF SLEEP

WEIGHT	BLOOD PRESSURE	BLOOD SUGAR

EXERCISE/ PHYSICAL ACTIVITY	SELF-CARE ACTIVITY

I will lay aside every weight, and sin, which tries to cling so closely to me.
(Hebrews 12:1)

DAY 42	SU MO TU WE TH FR SA	How Do I Feel Today
	DATE: ______________	☐ ☐ ☐ ☐

BREAKFAST	LUNCH	DINNER

SNACKS:

TOTAL CALORIES	GLASSES OF WATER	HOURS OF SLEEP

WEIGHT	BLOOD PRESSURE	BLOOD SUGAR

EXERCISE/ PHYSICAL ACTIVITY	SELF-CARE ACTIVITY

I will fix my eyes on Jesus, the founder and perfecter of my faith.
(Hebrews 12: 2)

DAY 43	SU MO TU WE TH FR SA DATE: ____________	How Do I Feel Today

BREAKFAST	LUNCH	DINNER

SNACKS:

TOTAL CALORIES	GLASSES OF WATER	HOURS OF SLEEP

WEIGHT	BLOOD PRESSURE	BLOOD SUGAR

EXERCISE/ PHYSICAL ACTIVITY	SELF-CARE ACTIVITY

When the righteous cry for help, the Lord hears, and rescues them from all their troubles.
(Psalm 34:17)

DAY 44	SU MO TU WE TH FR SA DATE: ________________	How Do I Feel Today ☐ ☐ ☐ ☐
BREAKFAST	LUNCH	DINNER

SNACKS:

TOTAL CALORIES	GLASSES OF WATER	HOURS OF SLEEP

WEIGHT	BLOOD PRESSURE	BLOOD SUGAR

EXERCISE/ PHYSICAL ACTIVITY	SELF-CARE ACTIVITY

I was bought with a price. Therefore, I will glorify God with my body.
(1 Corinthians 6:20)

DAY 45	SU MO TU WE TH FR SA DATE: ________________	How Do I Feel Today ☐ ☐ ☐ ☐

BREAKFAST	LUNCH	DINNER

SNACKS:

TOTAL CALORIES	GLASSES OF WATER	HOURS OF SLEEP

WEIGHT	BLOOD PRESSURE	BLOOD SUGAR

EXERCISE/ PHYSICAL ACTIVITY	SELF-CARE ACTIVITY

Peace of mind makes the body healthy; but envy rots the bones.
(*Proverbs* 14:30)

DAY 46	SU MO TU WE TH FR SA DATE: ______________	How Do I Feel Today ☐ ☐ ☐ ☐
BREAKFAST	LUNCH	DINNER

SNACKS:

TOTAL CALORIES	GLASSES OF WATER	HOURS OF SLEEP

WEIGHT	BLOOD PRESSURE	BLOOD SUGAR

EXERCISE/ PHYSICAL ACTIVITY	SELF-CARE ACTIVITY

I will show love for others by truly helping them, and not merely talk about it.
(1 John 3:18)

DAY 47	SU MO TU WE TH FR SA DATE: ______________	How Do I Feel Today

BREAKFAST	LUNCH	DINNER

SNACKS:

TOTAL CALORIES	GLASSES OF WATER	HOURS OF SLEEP

WEIGHT	BLOOD PRESSURE	BLOOD SUGAR

EXERCISE/ PHYSICAL ACTIVITY	SELF-CARE ACTIVITY

For God gave me a spirit, not of fear, but of power and love and self-control.
(2 Timothy 1:7)

DAY 48

SU MO TU WE TH FR SA

DATE: ____________

How Do I Feel Today

BREAKFAST	LUNCH	DINNER

SNACKS:

TOTAL CALORIES	GLASSES OF WATER	HOURS OF SLEEP

WEIGHT	BLOOD PRESSURE	BLOOD SUGAR

EXERCISE/ PHYSICAL ACTIVITY	SELF-CARE ACTIVITY

I will be happy in the Lord, and he will give me my heart's desire.
(Psalm 37:4)

DAY 49

SU MO TU WE TH FR SA

DATE: ____________________

How Do I Feel Today

☐ ☐ ☐ ☐

BREAKFAST	LUNCH	DINNER

SNACKS:

TOTAL CALORIES	GLASSES OF WATER	HOURS OF SLEEP

WEIGHT	BLOOD PRESSURE	BLOOD SUGAR

EXERCISE/ PHYSICAL ACTIVITY	SELF-CARE ACTIVITY

Man shall not live by bread alone, but by every word that comes from the mouth of God.
(Matthew 4:4)

DAY 50

SU MO TU WE TH FR SA

DATE: ______________

How Do I Feel Today

☐ ☐ ☐ ☐

BREAKFAST	LUNCH	DINNER

SNACKS:

TOTAL CALORIES	GLASSES OF WATER	HOURS OF SLEEP

WEIGHT	BLOOD PRESSURE	BLOOD SUGAR

EXERCISE/ PHYSICAL ACTIVITY	SELF-CARE ACTIVITY

The Lord is near to all who call on him. He fulfills the desires of those who fear him; he hears their cry and saves them. (Psalm 145: 18-19)

DAY 51

SU MO TU WE TH FR SA

DATE: ____________________

How Do I Feel Today

☐ ☐ ☐ ☐

BREAKFAST	LUNCH	DINNER

SNACKS:

TOTAL CALORIES	**GLASSES OF WATER**	**HOURS OF SLEEP**

WEIGHT	**BLOOD PRESSURE**	**BLOOD SUGAR**

EXERCISE/ PHYSICAL ACTIVITY	**SELF-CARE ACTIVITY**

I was made in the image and likeness of God.
(Genesis 1:26)

DAY 52	SU MO TU WE TH FR SA DATE: ______________	How Do I Feel Today

BREAKFAST	LUNCH	DINNER

SNACKS:

TOTAL CALORIES	GLASSES OF WATER	HOURS OF SLEEP

WEIGHT	BLOOD PRESSURE	BLOOD SUGAR

EXERCISE/ PHYSICAL ACTIVITY	SELF-CARE ACTIVITY

I was made to have dominion over all the Earth and over every living thing that creeps on the earth.
(Genesis 1:26)

DAY 53	SU MO TU WE TH FR SA DATE: ________	How Do I Feel Today ☐ ☐ ☐ ☐
BREAKFAST	LUNCH	DINNER
SNACKS:		
TOTAL CALORIES	GLASSES OF WATER	HOURS OF SLEEP
WEIGHT	BLOOD PRESSURE	BLOOD SUGAR
EXERCISE/ PHYSICAL ACTIVITY	SELF-CARE ACTIVITY	

From Him my whole body is fitted and held together by every supporting ligament; and as each individual part does its work, my body will grow and build itself up in love. (Ephesians 4:16)

DAY 54

SU MO TU WE TH FR SA

DATE: ______________

How Do I Feel Today

☐ ☐ ☐ ☐

BREAKFAST	LUNCH	DINNER

SNACKS:

TOTAL CALORIES	GLASSES OF WATER	HOURS OF SLEEP

WEIGHT	BLOOD PRESSURE	BLOOD SUGAR

EXERCISE/ PHYSICAL ACTIVITY	SELF-CARE ACTIVITY

I will grow to become in every respect the mature body of Christ, who is the head of my life.
(Ephesians 4:15)

DAY 55	SU MO TU WE TH FR SA DATE: ______________	How Do I Feel Today ☐ ☐ ☐ ☐
BREAKFAST	**LUNCH**	**DINNER**

SNACKS:

TOTAL CALORIES	GLASSES OF WATER	HOURS OF SLEEP

WEIGHT	BLOOD PRESSURE	BLOOD SUGAR

EXERCISE/ PHYSICAL ACTIVITY	SELF-CARE ACTIVITY

Jesus came, so that I will have life and have it more abundantly.
(John 10:10)

DAY 56	SU MO TU WE TH FR SA DATE: ____________	How Do I Feel Today

BREAKFAST	LUNCH	DINNER

SNACKS:

TOTAL CALORIES	GLASSES OF WATER	HOURS OF SLEEP

WEIGHT	BLOOD PRESSURE	BLOOD SUGAR

EXERCISE/ PHYSICAL ACTIVITY	SELF-CARE ACTIVITY

Daniel resolved that he would not defile himself with the king's food, or with the wine that he drank.
(*Daniel* 1:8)

DAY 57	SU MO TU WE TH FR SA DATE: ____________	How Do I Feel Today

BREAKFAST	LUNCH	DINNER

SNACKS:

TOTAL CALORIES	GLASSES OF WATER	HOURS OF SLEEP

WEIGHT	BLOOD PRESSURE	BLOOD SUGAR

EXERCISE/ PHYSICAL ACTIVITY	SELF-CARE ACTIVITY

For God is working in me, giving me the desire and the power to do what pleases him.
(Philippians 2:13)

DAY 58	SU MO TU WE TH FR SA DATE: ________________	How Do I Feel Today ☐ ☐ ☐ ☐
BREAKFAST	LUNCH	DINNER

SNACKS:

TOTAL CALORIES	GLASSES OF WATER	HOURS OF SLEEP

WEIGHT	BLOOD PRESSURE	BLOOD SUGAR

EXERCISE/ PHYSICAL ACTIVITY	SELF-CARE ACTIVITY

I will approach the throne of grace with boldness, so that I will receive mercy and find grace to help me in times of need. (Hebrews 4:16)

DAY 59	SU MO TU WE TH FR SA DATE: ______________	How Do I Feel Today

BREAKFAST	LUNCH	DINNER

SNACKS:

TOTAL CALORIES	GLASSES OF WATER	HOURS OF SLEEP

WEIGHT	BLOOD PRESSURE	BLOOD SUGAR

EXERCISE/ PHYSICAL ACTIVITY	SELF-CARE ACTIVITY

The earnest prayer of a righteous person is powerful and effective.
(James 5:16)

DAY 60	SU MO TU WE TH FR SA DATE: ____________	How Do I Feel Today ☐ ☐ ☐ ☐

BREAKFAST	LUNCH	DINNER

SNACKS:

TOTAL CALORIES	GLASSES OF WATER	HOURS OF SLEEP

WEIGHT	BLOOD PRESSURE	BLOOD SUGAR

EXERCISE/ PHYSICAL ACTIVITY	SELF-CARE ACTIVITY

With God all things are possible.
(Luke 1:37)

DAY 61

SU MO TU WE TH FR SA

DATE: ____________

How Do I Feel Today

☐ ☐ ☐ ☐

BREAKFAST	LUNCH	DINNER

SNACKS:

TOTAL CALORIES	GLASSES OF WATER	HOURS OF SLEEP

WEIGHT	BLOOD PRESSURE	BLOOD SUGAR

EXERCISE/ PHYSICAL ACTIVITY	SELF-CARE ACTIVITY

I will put away, anger, wrath, malice, slander, and obscene talk from your mouth.
(Colossians 3:8)

DAY 62	SU MO TU WE TH FR SA DATE: ____________	How Do I Feel Today ☐ ☐ ☐ ☐

BREAKFAST	LUNCH	DINNER

SNACKS:

TOTAL CALORIES	GLASSES OF WATER	HOURS OF SLEEP

WEIGHT	BLOOD PRESSURE	BLOOD SUGAR

EXERCISE/ PHYSICAL ACTIVITY	SELF-CARE ACTIVITY

In all labor there is profit, But mere talk leads only to poverty.
(Proverbs 14:23)

DAY 63

SU MO TU WE TH FR SA

DATE: ____________________

How Do I Feel Today

BREAKFAST	LUNCH	DINNER

SNACKS:

TOTAL CALORIES	GLASSES OF WATER	HOURS OF SLEEP

WEIGHT	BLOOD PRESSURE	BLOOD SUGAR

EXERCISE/ PHYSICAL ACTIVITY	SELF-CARE ACTIVITY

The Lord will help me and rescue me; he will deliver me from all evil, because, I seek his protection.
(Psalm 37:40)

DAY 64

SU MO TU WE TH FR SA

DATE: ____________________

How Do I Feel Today

☐ ☐ ☐ ☐

BREAKFAST	LUNCH	DINNER

SNACKS:

TOTAL CALORIES	GLASSES OF WATER	HOURS OF SLEEP

WEIGHT	BLOOD PRESSURE	BLOOD SUGAR

EXERCISE/ PHYSICAL ACTIVITY	SELF-CARE ACTIVITY

The Lord rescues the godly; he is my stronghold in times of trouble.
(Psalms 37:39)

DAY 65	SU MO TU WE TH FR SA DATE: ______________	How Do I Feel Today ☐ ☐ ☐ ☐
BREAKFAST	LUNCH	DINNER

SNACKS:

TOTAL CALORIES	GLASSES OF WATER	HOURS OF SLEEP

WEIGHT	BLOOD PRESSURE	BLOOD SUGAR

EXERCISE/ PHYSICAL ACTIVITY	SELF-CARE ACTIVITY

A great future awaits those who love peace. (Psalm 37:37)

DAY 66	SU MO TU WE TH FR SA DATE: ______________	How Do I Feel Today ☐ ☐ ☐ ☐

BREAKFAST	LUNCH	DINNER

SNACKS:

TOTAL CALORIES	GLASSES OF WATER	HOURS OF SLEEP

WEIGHT	BLOOD PRESSURE	BLOOD SUGAR

EXERCISE/ PHYSICAL ACTIVITY	SELF-CARE ACTIVITY

The word of God is alive and powerful! It is sharper than any double-edged sword.
(Hebrews 4:12)

DAY 67	SU MO TU WE TH FR SA DATE: ____________	How Do I Feel Today ☐ ☐ ☐ ☐

BREAKFAST	LUNCH	DINNER

SNACKS:

TOTAL CALORIES	GLASSES OF WATER	HOURS OF SLEEP

WEIGHT	BLOOD PRESSURE	BLOOD SUGAR

EXERCISE/ PHYSICAL ACTIVITY	SELF-CARE ACTIVITY

Lord, you alone deserves all of the praise, because of your love and faithfulness.
(Psalm 115:1)

DAY 68

SU MO TU WE TH FR SA

DATE: ____________________

How Do I Feel Today

BREAKFAST	LUNCH	DINNER

SNACKS:

TOTAL CALORIES	GLASSES OF WATER	HOURS OF SLEEP

WEIGHT	BLOOD PRESSURE	BLOOD SUGAR

EXERCISE/ PHYSICAL ACTIVITY	SELF-CARE ACTIVITY

I will extol the Lord, both now and forevermore. Praise the Lord!
(*Psalm* 115:18)

DAY 69	SU MO TU WE TH FR SA DATE: ____________	How Do I Feel Today ☐ ☐ ☐ ☐

BREAKFAST	LUNCH	DINNER

SNACKS:

TOTAL CALORIES	GLASSES OF WATER	HOURS OF SLEEP

WEIGHT	BLOOD PRESSURE	BLOOD SUGAR

EXERCISE/ PHYSICAL ACTIVITY	SELF-CARE ACTIVITY

I am blessed by the Lord, the Maker of Heaven and Earth. (*Psalm* 115:15)

DAY 70

SU MO TU WE TH FR SA

DATE: ____________________

How Do I Feel Today

BREAKFAST	LUNCH	DINNER

SNACKS:

TOTAL CALORIES	**GLASSES OF WATER**	**HOURS OF SLEEP**

WEIGHT	**BLOOD PRESSURE**	**BLOOD SUGAR**

EXERCISE/ PHYSICAL ACTIVITY	**SELF-CARE ACTIVITY**

He will not allow any disease to overtake me, for He is the Lord, my healer.
(Exodus 15:26)

DAY 71	SU MO TU WE TH FR SA DATE: ____________	How Do I Feel Today ☐ ☐ ☐ ☐
BREAKFAST	LUNCH	DINNER

SNACKS:

TOTAL CALORIES	GLASSES OF WATER	HOURS OF SLEEP

WEIGHT	BLOOD PRESSURE	BLOOD SUGAR

EXERCISE/ PHYSICAL ACTIVITY	SELF-CARE ACTIVITY

His blessing will be on my food and water and He will take away sickness from me.
(Exodus 23:25)

DAY 72	SU MO TU WE TH FR SA DATE: ________________	How Do I Feel Today ☐ ☐ ☐ ☐

BREAKFAST	LUNCH	DINNER

SNACKS:

TOTAL CALORIES	GLASSES OF WATER	HOURS OF SLEEP

WEIGHT	BLOOD PRESSURE	BLOOD SUGAR

EXERCISE/ PHYSICAL ACTIVITY	SELF-CARE ACTIVITY

I will not fear for God is with you; I will not be dismayed, for He is my God.
He will strengthen me and help me; He will uphold me with His righteous right hand.
(*Isaiah* 41:10)

DAY 73	SU MO TU WE TH FR SA DATE: ____________	How Do I Feel Today ☐ ☐ ☐ ☐
BREAKFAST	LUNCH	DINNER

SNACKS:

TOTAL CALORIES	GLASSES OF WATER	HOURS OF SLEEP

WEIGHT	BLOOD PRESSURE	BLOOD SUGAR

EXERCISE/ PHYSICAL ACTIVITY	SELF-CARE ACTIVITY

By His wounds I am healed.
(Isaiah 53:5)

DAY 74	SU MO TU WE TH FR SA DATE: ____________	How Do I Feel Today ☐ ☐ ☐ ☐
BREAKFAST	LUNCH	DINNER

SNACKS:

TOTAL CALORIES	GLASSES OF WATER	HOURS OF SLEEP

WEIGHT	BLOOD PRESSURE	BLOOD SUGAR

EXERCISE/ PHYSICAL ACTIVITY	SELF-CARE ACTIVITY

He gives strength to the weary and increases the power of the weak.
(Isaiah 40:29)

DAY 75	SU MO TU WE (TH) FR SA DATE: 5/29/25	How Do I Feel Today

BREAKFAST	LUNCH	DINNER
Fasted	Fasted	Tortilla coconut rice sourdough

SNACKS:

TOTAL CALORIES	GLASSES OF WATER	HOURS OF SLEEP

WEIGHT	BLOOD PRESSURE	BLOOD SUGAR

EXERCISE/ PHYSICAL ACTIVITY	SELF-CARE ACTIVITY

When I am tempted, He will provide a way out, so that, I will be able to endure it.
(1 Corinthians 10:13)

DAY 76

SU MO TU WE TH (FR) SA

DATE: 5/30/25

How Do I Feel Today

BREAKFAST	LUNCH	DINNER
sourdough eggs Avo		

SNACKS:

TOTAL CALORIES	GLASSES OF WATER	HOURS OF SLEEP

WEIGHT	BLOOD PRESSURE	BLOOD SUGAR

EXERCISE/ PHYSICAL ACTIVITY	SELF-CARE ACTIVITY

2pm - anxious

The Lord redeems my life from the pit and crowns me with love and compassion.
(Psalms 103:4)

DAY 77	SU MO TU WE TH FR SA DATE: ______________	How Do I Feel Today ☐ ☐ ☐ ☐
BREAKFAST	LUNCH	DINNER

SNACKS:

TOTAL CALORIES	**GLASSES OF WATER**	**HOURS OF SLEEP**
WEIGHT	**BLOOD PRESSURE**	**BLOOD SUGAR**

EXERCISE/ PHYSICAL ACTIVITY	**SELF-CARE ACTIVITY**

My heart rejoices in Your salvation, oh Lord. (Psalm 13:5)

DAY 78	SU MO TU WE TH FR SA DATE: ______	How Do I Feel Today ☐ ☐ ☐ ☐
BREAKFAST	LUNCH	DINNER

SNACKS:

TOTAL CALORIES	GLASSES OF WATER	HOURS OF SLEEP

WEIGHT	BLOOD PRESSURE	BLOOD SUGAR

EXERCISE/ PHYSICAL ACTIVITY	SELF-CARE ACTIVITY

I trust in your unfailing love, oh Lord. (*Psalm 13:5*)

DAY 79

SU MO TU WE TH FR SA

DATE: ____________________

How Do I Feel Today

BREAKFAST	LUNCH	DINNER

SNACKS:

TOTAL CALORIES	**GLASSES OF WATER**	**HOURS OF SLEEP**

WEIGHT	**BLOOD PRESSURE**	**BLOOD SUGAR**

EXERCISE/ PHYSICAL ACTIVITY	**SELF-CARE ACTIVITY**

He will satisfy me with a long life, And show me His salvation. (Psalm 91:16)

DAY 80	SU MO TU WE TH FR SA DATE: ______________	How Do I Feel Today ☐ ☐ ☐ ☐
BREAKFAST	LUNCH	DINNER

SNACKS:

TOTAL CALORIES	GLASSES OF WATER	HOURS OF SLEEP

WEIGHT	BLOOD PRESSURE	BLOOD SUGAR

EXERCISE/ PHYSICAL ACTIVITY	SELF-CARE ACTIVITY

The Lord is my strength and song, And He has become my salvation.
(*Psalm* 118:14)

DAY 81

SU MO TU WE TH FR SA

DATE: ____________________

How Do I Feel Today

☐ ☐ ☐ ☐

BREAKFAST	LUNCH	DINNER

SNACKS:

TOTAL CALORIES	**GLASSES OF WATER**	**HOURS OF SLEEP**

WEIGHT	**BLOOD PRESSURE**	**BLOOD SUGAR**

EXERCISE/ PHYSICAL ACTIVITY	**SELF-CARE ACTIVITY**

God is my salvation, I will trust in Him and not be afraid. (Isaiah 12:2)

DAY 82	SU MO TU WE TH FR SA DATE: ____________	How Do I Feel Today ☐ ☐ ☐ ☐

BREAKFAST	LUNCH	DINNER

SNACKS:

TOTAL CALORIES	GLASSES OF WATER	HOURS OF SLEEP

WEIGHT	BLOOD PRESSURE	BLOOD SUGAR

EXERCISE/ PHYSICAL ACTIVITY	SELF-CARE ACTIVITY

The Lord himself, is my strength and my defense. He will always come to my rescue.
(*Isaiah* 12:2)

DAY 83	SU MO TU WE TH FR SA DATE: ____________	How Do I Feel Today ☐ ☐ ☐ ☐

BREAKFAST	LUNCH	DINNER

SNACKS:

TOTAL CALORIES	GLASSES OF WATER	HOURS OF SLEEP

WEIGHT	BLOOD PRESSURE	BLOOD SUGAR

EXERCISE/ PHYSICAL ACTIVITY	SELF-CARE ACTIVITY

The Lord will sanctify me completely. He will preserve my spirit, soul and body.
(1 Thessalonian 5:23)

DAY 84

SU MO TU WE TH FR SA

DATE: ___________________

How Do I Feel Today

☐ ☐ ☐ ☐

BREAKFAST	LUNCH	DINNER

SNACKS:

TOTAL CALORIES	GLASSES OF WATER	HOURS OF SLEEP

WEIGHT	BLOOD PRESSURE	BLOOD SUGAR

EXERCISE/ PHYSICAL ACTIVITY	SELF-CARE ACTIVITY

I will have a long life; His peace will be upon me, upon my family, and upon all my possessions.
(1 Samuel 25:6)

DAY 85

SU MO TU WE TH FR SA

DATE: ____________

How Do I Feel Today

☐ ☐ ☐ ☐

BREAKFAST	LUNCH	DINNER

SNACKS:

TOTAL CALORIES	GLASSES OF WATER	HOURS OF SLEEP

WEIGHT	BLOOD PRESSURE	BLOOD SUGAR

EXERCISE/ PHYSICAL ACTIVITY	SELF-CARE ACTIVITY

The Lord will bring health and healing to my body, and will reveal to me an abundance of peace and truth. (Jeremiah 33:6)

DAY 86	SU MO TU WE TH FR SA DATE: ______________	How Do I Feel Today ☐ ☐ ☐ ☐

BREAKFAST	LUNCH	DINNER

SNACKS:

TOTAL CALORIES	GLASSES OF WATER	HOURS OF SLEEP

WEIGHT	BLOOD PRESSURE	BLOOD SUGAR

EXERCISE/ PHYSICAL ACTIVITY	SELF-CARE ACTIVITY

I will keep His words in the midst of my heart. For they will give life and good health to my body.
(Proverbs 4:20 - 22)

DAY 87	SU MO TU WE TH FR SA DATE: ____________	How Do I Feel Today ☐ ☐ ☐ ☐
BREAKFAST	LUNCH	DINNER

SNACKS:

TOTAL CALORIES	GLASSES OF WATER	HOURS OF SLEEP

WEIGHT	BLOOD PRESSURE	BLOOD SUGAR

EXERCISE/ PHYSICAL ACTIVITY	SELF-CARE ACTIVITY

Godliness is profitable for all things, since it holds promise for the present life and also for the life to come. (1 Timothy 4:8)

DAY 88

SU MO TU WE TH FR SA

DATE: ____________

How Do I Feel Today ☐ ☐ ☐ ☐

BREAKFAST	LUNCH	DINNER

SNACKS:

TOTAL CALORIES	GLASSES OF WATER	HOURS OF SLEEP

WEIGHT	BLOOD PRESSURE	BLOOD SUGAR

EXERCISE/ PHYSICAL ACTIVITY	SELF-CARE ACTIVITY

The steadfast love of the LORD never ceases; his mercies never come to an end; they are new every morning; great is His faithfulness. (*Lamentations 3:22-23:*)

DAY 89	SU MO TU WE TH FR SA DATE: ______________	How Do I Feel Today ☐ ☐ ☐ ☐

BREAKFAST	LUNCH	DINNER

SNACKS:

TOTAL CALORIES	GLASSES OF WATER	HOURS OF SLEEP

WEIGHT	BLOOD PRESSURE	BLOOD SUGAR

EXERCISE/ PHYSICAL ACTIVITY	SELF-CARE ACTIVITY

The name of the LORD is a strong tower; the righteous runs into it and is safe.
(*Proverbs* 18:10)

DAY 90

SU MO TU WE TH FR SA

DATE: ____________________

How Do I Feel Today

BREAKFAST	LUNCH	DINNER

SNACKS:

TOTAL CALORIES	GLASSES OF WATER	HOURS OF SLEEP

WEIGHT	BLOOD PRESSURE	BLOOD SUGAR

EXERCISE/ PHYSICAL ACTIVITY	SELF-CARE ACTIVITY

The Lord lives! Praise to my Rock! May God, the Rock of my salvation, be exalted!
(2 Samuel 22:47)

DAY 91	SU MO TU WE TH FR SA DATE: ____________	How Do I Feel Today ☐ ☐ ☐ ☐

BREAKFAST	LUNCH	DINNER

SNACKS:

TOTAL CALORIES	GLASSES OF WATER	HOURS OF SLEEP

WEIGHT	BLOOD PRESSURE	BLOOD SUGAR

EXERCISE/ PHYSICAL ACTIVITY	SELF-CARE ACTIVITY

The Lord almighty is with me; the God of Jacob is my fortress.
(*Psalm 46:7*)

DAY 92	SU MO TU WE TH FR SA DATE: ______________	How Do I Feel Today ☐ ☐ ☐ ☐

BREAKFAST	LUNCH	DINNER

SNACKS:

TOTAL CALORIES	GLASSES OF WATER	HOURS OF SLEEP

WEIGHT	BLOOD PRESSURE	BLOOD SUGAR

EXERCISE/ PHYSICAL ACTIVITY	SELF-CARE ACTIVITY

I will cast my burdens on the Lord, for he will sustain me; he will never let me be defeated.
(*Psalm 55:22*)

DAY 93	SU MO TU WE TH FR SA DATE: ______________	How Do I Feel Today ☐ ☐ ☐ ☐
BREAKFAST	LUNCH	DINNER

SNACKS:

TOTAL CALORIES	GLASSES OF WATER	HOURS OF SLEEP

WEIGHT	BLOOD PRESSURE	BLOOD SUGAR

EXERCISE/ PHYSICAL ACTIVITY	SELF-CARE ACTIVITY

The Lord is my rock and my salvation, He is my fortress; I shall not be shaken.
(Psalm 62:6)

DAY 94	SU MO TU WE TH FR SA DATE: ______________	How Do I Feel Today ☐ ☐ ☐ ☐

BREAKFAST	LUNCH	DINNER

SNACKS:

TOTAL CALORIES	GLASSES OF WATER	HOURS OF SLEEP

WEIGHT	BLOOD PRESSURE	BLOOD SUGAR

EXERCISE/ PHYSICAL ACTIVITY	SELF-CARE ACTIVITY

Lord, You are my refuge and my shield; I have put my hope in your word.
(Psalm 119:114)

DAY 95

SU MO TU WE TH FR SA

DATE: ______________

How Do I Feel Today

BREAKFAST	LUNCH	DINNER

SNACKS:

TOTAL CALORIES	GLASSES OF WATER	HOURS OF SLEEP

WEIGHT	BLOOD PRESSURE	BLOOD SUGAR

EXERCISE/ PHYSICAL ACTIVITY	SELF-CARE ACTIVITY

The Lord is faithful. He will strengthen me and protect me from evil.
(2 Thessalonians 3:3)

DAY 96	SU MO TU WE TH FR SA DATE: ____________	How Do I Feel Today ☐ ☐ ☐ ☐
BREAKFAST	LUNCH	DINNER

SNACKS:

TOTAL CALORIES	GLASSES OF WATER	HOURS OF SLEEP

WEIGHT	BLOOD PRESSURE	BLOOD SUGAR

EXERCISE/ PHYSICAL ACTIVITY	SELF-CARE ACTIVITY

I will go out with joy and be led forth with peace. (Isaiah 55:12)

DAY 97	SU MO TU WE TH FR SA DATE: ____________	How Do I Feel Today ☐ ☐ ☐ ☐

BREAKFAST	LUNCH	DINNER

SNACKS:

TOTAL CALORIES	GLASSES OF WATER	HOURS OF SLEEP

WEIGHT	BLOOD PRESSURE	BLOOD SUGAR

EXERCISE/ PHYSICAL ACTIVITY	SELF-CARE ACTIVITY

Surely your goodness and love will follow me all the days of my life. (Psalm 23:6)

DAY 98	SU MO TU WE TH FR SA DATE: ______________	How Do I Feel Today ☐ ☐ ☐ ☐
BREAKFAST	LUNCH	DINNER

SNACKS:

TOTAL CALORIES	GLASSES OF WATER	HOURS OF SLEEP

WEIGHT	BLOOD PRESSURE	BLOOD SUGAR

EXERCISE/ PHYSICAL ACTIVITY	SELF-CARE ACTIVITY

The hope of the righteous brings joy, but the expectation of the wicked will perish.
(Proverbs 10:28)

DAY 99	SU MO TU WE TH FR SA DATE: ______________	How Do I Feel Today ☐ ☐ ☐ ☐

BREAKFAST	LUNCH	DINNER

SNACKS:

TOTAL CALORIES	GLASSES OF WATER	HOURS OF SLEEP

WEIGHT	BLOOD PRESSURE	BLOOD SUGAR

EXERCISE/ PHYSICAL ACTIVITY	SELF-CARE ACTIVITY

I will Rejoice always, pray without ceasing, and give thanks in all circumstances;
For this is the will of God in Christ Jesus for me. (1 Thessalonians 5:16-18)

DAY 100	SU MO TU WE TH FR SA DATE: ______________	How Do I Feel Today ☐ ☐ ☐ ☐

BREAKFAST	LUNCH	DINNER

SNACKS:

TOTAL CALORIES	GLASSES OF WATER	HOURS OF SLEEP

WEIGHT	BLOOD PRESSURE	BLOOD SUGAR

EXERCISE/ PHYSICAL ACTIVITY	SELF-CARE ACTIVITY

My heart is glad, my whole being rejoices and my flesh also dwells secure.
(*Psalm* 16:9)

DAY 101

SU MO TU WE TH FR SA

DATE: ____________________

How Do I Feel Today

BREAKFAST	LUNCH	DINNER

SNACKS:

TOTAL CALORIES	GLASSES OF WATER	HOURS OF SLEEP

WEIGHT	BLOOD PRESSURE	BLOOD SUGAR

EXERCISE/ PHYSICAL ACTIVITY	SELF-CARE ACTIVITY

For his anger is but for a moment, and his favor is for a lifetime. (Psalm 30:5)

DAY 102	SU MO TU WE TH FR SA DATE: ____________	How Do I Feel Today ☐ ☐ ☐ ☐

BREAKFAST	LUNCH	DINNER

SNACKS:

TOTAL CALORIES	GLASSES OF WATER	HOURS OF SLEEP

WEIGHT	BLOOD PRESSURE	BLOOD SUGAR

EXERCISE/ PHYSICAL ACTIVITY	SELF-CARE ACTIVITY

Weeping may tarry for the night, but joy comes with the morning. (Psalm 30:5)

DAY 103

SU MO TU WE TH FR SA

DATE: ____________________

How Do I Feel Today

☐ ☐ ☐ ☐

BREAKFAST	LUNCH	DINNER

SNACKS:

TOTAL CALORIES	GLASSES OF WATER	HOURS OF SLEEP

WEIGHT	BLOOD PRESSURE	BLOOD SUGAR

EXERCISE/ PHYSICAL ACTIVITY	SELF-CARE ACTIVITY

You make known to me the path of life; in your presence there is fullness of joy; at your right hand are pleasures forevermore. (Psalm 16:11)

DAY 104

SU MO TU WE TH FR SA

DATE: ____________________

How Do I Feel Today

☐ ☐ ☐ ☐

BREAKFAST	LUNCH	DINNER

SNACKS:

TOTAL CALORIES	GLASSES OF WATER	HOURS OF SLEEP

WEIGHT	BLOOD PRESSURE	BLOOD SUGAR

EXERCISE/ PHYSICAL ACTIVITY	SELF-CARE ACTIVITY

This is the day that the Lord has made; I will rejoice and be glad in it.
(*Psalm* 118:24)

DAY 105

SU MO TU WE TH FR SA

DATE: ____________________

How Do I Feel Today

BREAKFAST	LUNCH	DINNER

SNACKS:

TOTAL CALORIES	**GLASSES OF WATER**	**HOURS OF SLEEP**

WEIGHT	**BLOOD PRESSURE**	**BLOOD SUGAR**

EXERCISE/ PHYSICAL ACTIVITY	**SELF-CARE ACTIVITY**

Send me your light and your faithful care, let them lead me, oh Lord. (Psalm 43:3)

DAY 106

SU MO TU WE TH FR SA

DATE: ____________________

How Do I Feel Today

BREAKFAST	LUNCH	DINNER

SNACKS:

TOTAL CALORIES	GLASSES OF WATER	HOURS OF SLEEP

WEIGHT	BLOOD PRESSURE	BLOOD SUGAR

EXERCISE/ PHYSICAL ACTIVITY	SELF-CARE ACTIVITY

For He shall give His angels charge over me, to keep me in all my ways. (Psalm 91:11)

DAY 107

SU MO TU WE TH FR SA

DATE: ____________________

How Do I Feel Today

BREAKFAST	LUNCH	DINNER

SNACKS:

TOTAL CALORIES	GLASSES OF WATER	HOURS OF SLEEP

WEIGHT	BLOOD PRESSURE	BLOOD SUGAR

EXERCISE/ PHYSICAL ACTIVITY	SELF-CARE ACTIVITY

Whatever I ask for, in the name of Jesus, I will receive, so that my joy may be complete. (John 16:24)

DAY 108

SU MO TU WE TH FR SA

DATE: ____________

How Do I Feel Today

☐ ☐ ☐ ☐

BREAKFAST	LUNCH	DINNER

SNACKS:

TOTAL CALORIES	GLASSES OF WATER	HOURS OF SLEEP

WEIGHT	BLOOD PRESSURE	BLOOD SUGAR

EXERCISE/ PHYSICAL ACTIVITY	SELF-CARE ACTIVITY

I possess the fruits of the Spirit: I have love, joy, peace, patience, kindness, goodness, faithfulness, gentleness and self-control. (Galatians 5:22-23)

DAY 109

SU MO TU WE TH FR SA

DATE: ____________________

How Do I Feel Today

☐ ☐ ☐ ☐

BREAKFAST	LUNCH	DINNER

SNACKS:

TOTAL CALORIES	GLASSES OF WATER	HOURS OF SLEEP

WEIGHT	BLOOD PRESSURE	BLOOD SUGAR

EXERCISE/ PHYSICAL ACTIVITY	SELF-CARE ACTIVITY

I will consider it pure joy, whenever I face trials of any kind, because I know that the testing of my faith produces perseverance. (James 1:2-3)

DAY 110	SU MO TU WE TH FR SA DATE: ______________	How Do I Feel Today

BREAKFAST	LUNCH	DINNER

SNACKS:

TOTAL CALORIES	GLASSES OF WATER	HOURS OF SLEEP

WEIGHT	BLOOD PRESSURE	BLOOD SUGAR

EXERCISE/ PHYSICAL ACTIVITY	SELF-CARE ACTIVITY

May the God of hope fill me with joy and peace in believing, so that by the power of the Holy Spirit I may abound in hope. (Romans 15:13)

DAY 111

SU MO TU WE TH FR SA

DATE: ____________

How Do I Feel Today

BREAKFAST	LUNCH	DINNER

SNACKS:

TOTAL CALORIES	**GLASSES OF WATER**	**HOURS OF SLEEP**

WEIGHT	**BLOOD PRESSURE**	**BLOOD SUGAR**

EXERCISE/ PHYSICAL ACTIVITY	**SELF-CARE ACTIVITY**

My peace comes from the Lord, so my heart will not be troubled, and I will not be afraid.
(John 14:27)

DAY 112	SU MO TU WE TH FR SA DATE: ________________	How Do I Feel Today

BREAKFAST	LUNCH	DINNER

SNACKS:

TOTAL CALORIES	GLASSES OF WATER	HOURS OF SLEEP

WEIGHT	BLOOD PRESSURE	BLOOD SUGAR

EXERCISE/ PHYSICAL ACTIVITY	SELF-CARE ACTIVITY

Splendor and majesty are before the Lord; strength and joy are in his place.
(1 Chronicles 16:27)

DAY 113

SU MO TU WE TH FR SA

DATE: ____________________

How Do I Feel Today

BREAKFAST	LUNCH	DINNER

SNACKS:

TOTAL CALORIES	GLASSES OF WATER	HOURS OF SLEEP

WEIGHT	BLOOD PRESSURE	BLOOD SUGAR

EXERCISE/ PHYSICAL ACTIVITY	SELF-CARE ACTIVITY

You have turned for me my mourning into dancing; you have loosed my sackcloth and clothed me with gladness. (Psalm 30:11)

DAY 114

SU MO TU WE TH FR SA

DATE: ____________________

How Do I Feel Today

☐ ☐ ☐ ☐

BREAKFAST	LUNCH	DINNER

SNACKS:

TOTAL CALORIES	**GLASSES OF WATER**	**HOURS OF SLEEP**

WEIGHT	**BLOOD PRESSURE**	**BLOOD SUGAR**

EXERCISE/ PHYSICAL ACTIVITY	**SELF-CARE ACTIVITY**

I will look to Jesus, the founder and perfecter of my faith, who for the joy that was set before him endured the cross, despising the shame, and is seated at the right hand of the throne of God.
(Hebrews 12:2)

DAY 115	SU MO TU WE TH FR SA DATE: ____________	How Do I Feel Today ☐ ☐ ☐ ☐

BREAKFAST	LUNCH	DINNER

SNACKS:

TOTAL CALORIES	GLASSES OF WATER	HOURS OF SLEEP

WEIGHT	BLOOD PRESSURE	BLOOD SUGAR

EXERCISE/ PHYSICAL ACTIVITY	SELF-CARE ACTIVITY

All who take refuge in the Lord will rejoice; they will ever sing for joy, because you spread your protection over them, oh Lord; they will rejoice in you. (Psalm 5:11)

DAY 116

SU MO TU WE TH FR SA

DATE: ____________________

How Do I Feel Today

BREAKFAST	LUNCH	DINNER

SNACKS:

TOTAL CALORIES	GLASSES OF WATER	HOURS OF SLEEP

WEIGHT	BLOOD PRESSURE	BLOOD SUGAR

EXERCISE/ PHYSICAL ACTIVITY	SELF-CARE ACTIVITY

I will be strengthened with all power, according to his glorious might,
so that I will have great endurance and patience and joy. (Colossians 1:11)

DAY 117	SU MO TU WE TH FR SA DATE: ____________	How Do I Feel Today ☐ ☐ ☐ ☐

BREAKFAST	LUNCH	DINNER

SNACKS:

TOTAL CALORIES	GLASSES OF WATER	HOURS OF SLEEP

WEIGHT	BLOOD PRESSURE	BLOOD SUGAR

EXERCISE/ PHYSICAL ACTIVITY	SELF-CARE ACTIVITY

For I walk by faith, not by sight.
(2 Corinthians 5:7)

DAY 118

SU MO TU WE TH FR SA

DATE: ____________________

How Do I Feel Today

BREAKFAST	LUNCH	DINNER

SNACKS:

TOTAL CALORIES	GLASSES OF WATER	HOURS OF SLEEP

WEIGHT	BLOOD PRESSURE	BLOOD SUGAR

EXERCISE/ PHYSICAL ACTIVITY	SELF-CARE ACTIVITY

I will seek his will in all that I do, and he will show me which path to take.
(Proverbs 3:6)

DAY 119

SU MO TU WE TH FR SA

DATE: ____________________

How Do I Feel Today

BREAKFAST	LUNCH	DINNER

SNACKS:

TOTAL CALORIES	GLASSES OF WATER	HOURS OF SLEEP

WEIGHT	BLOOD PRESSURE	BLOOD SUGAR

EXERCISE/ PHYSICAL ACTIVITY	SELF-CARE ACTIVITY

With God, all things are possible. (Luke 1:37)

DAY 120

SU MO TU WE TH FR SA

DATE: ____________________

How Do I Feel Today

☐ ☐ ☐ ☐

BREAKFAST	LUNCH	DINNER

SNACKS:

TOTAL CALORIES	GLASSES OF WATER	HOURS OF SLEEP

WEIGHT	BLOOD PRESSURE	BLOOD SUGAR

EXERCISE/ PHYSICAL ACTIVITY	SELF-CARE ACTIVITY

Whatever I ask in prayer, I will believe that I have received it, and it will be mine. (Mark 11:24)

DAY 121	SU MO TU WE TH FR SA DATE: ______________	How Do I Feel Today ☐ ☐ ☐ ☐
BREAKFAST	LUNCH	DINNER

SNACKS:

TOTAL CALORIES	GLASSES OF WATER	HOURS OF SLEEP

WEIGHT	BLOOD PRESSURE	BLOOD SUGAR

EXERCISE/ PHYSICAL ACTIVITY	SELF-CARE ACTIVITY

Faith is the assurance of things hoped for, the conviction of things not seen. (Hebrews 11:1)

DAY 122	SU MO TU WE TH FR SA DATE: ________________	How Do I Feel Today ☐ ☐ ☐ ☐
BREAKFAST	LUNCH	DINNER
SNACKS:		
TOTAL CALORIES	GLASSES OF WATER	HOURS OF SLEEP
WEIGHT	BLOOD PRESSURE	BLOOD SUGAR
EXERCISE/ PHYSICAL ACTIVITY	SELF-CARE ACTIVITY	

Without faith it is impossible to please God, for whoever would draw near to God must believe that he exists and that he rewards those who seek him. (Hebrews 11:6)

DAY 123

SU MO TU WE TH FR SA

DATE: ____________________

How Do I Feel Today

BREAKFAST	LUNCH	DINNER

SNACKS:

TOTAL CALORIES	GLASSES OF WATER	HOURS OF SLEEP

WEIGHT	BLOOD PRESSURE	BLOOD SUGAR

EXERCISE/ PHYSICAL ACTIVITY	SELF-CARE ACTIVITY

Faith comes from hearing, and hearing through the word of Christ.
(Romans 10:17)

DAY 124	SU MO TU WE TH FR SA DATE: ____________	How Do I Feel Today ☐ ☐ ☐ ☐
BREAKFAST	LUNCH	DINNER

SNACKS:

TOTAL CALORIES	GLASSES OF WATER	HOURS OF SLEEP

WEIGHT	BLOOD PRESSURE	BLOOD SUGAR

EXERCISE/ PHYSICAL ACTIVITY	SELF-CARE ACTIVITY

Whatever I ask in prayer, I will receive it, because I have faith in Christ.
(Matthew 21:22)

DAY 125	SU MO TU WE TH FR SA DATE: ___________	How Do I Feel Today ☐ ☐ ☐ ☐

BREAKFAST	LUNCH	DINNER

SNACKS:

TOTAL CALORIES	GLASSES OF WATER	HOURS OF SLEEP

WEIGHT	BLOOD PRESSURE	BLOOD SUGAR

EXERCISE/ PHYSICAL ACTIVITY	SELF-CARE ACTIVITY

Love bears all things, believes all things, hopes all things, endures all things.
(1 Corinthians 13:7)

DAY 126

SU MO TU WE TH FR SA

DATE: ____________________

How Do I Feel Today

BREAKFAST	LUNCH	DINNER

SNACKS:

TOTAL CALORIES	GLASSES OF WATER	HOURS OF SLEEP

WEIGHT	BLOOD PRESSURE	BLOOD SUGAR

EXERCISE/ PHYSICAL ACTIVITY	SELF-CARE ACTIVITY

I am a child of God.
(1 John 3:1)

DAY 127	SU MO TU WE TH FR SA DATE: ____________	How Do I Feel Today ☐ ☐ ☐ ☐

BREAKFAST	LUNCH	DINNER

SNACKS:

TOTAL CALORIES	**GLASSES OF WATER**	**HOURS OF SLEEP**

WEIGHT	**BLOOD PRESSURE**	**BLOOD SUGAR**

EXERCISE/ PHYSICAL ACTIVITY	**SELF-CARE ACTIVITY**

God is love, and whoever abides in love abides in Christ, and Christ abides in him.
(1 John 4:16)

DAY 128	SU MO TU WE TH FR SA DATE: ____________	How Do I Feel Today

BREAKFAST	LUNCH	DINNER

SNACKS:

TOTAL CALORIES	GLASSES OF WATER	HOURS OF SLEEP

WEIGHT	BLOOD PRESSURE	BLOOD SUGAR

EXERCISE/ PHYSICAL ACTIVITY	SELF-CARE ACTIVITY

The Lord gives strength to his people; the Lord blesses his people with peace. (Psalm 29:11)

DAY 129

SU MO TU WE TH FR SA

DATE: ____________________

How Do I Feel Today

☐ ☐ ☐ ☐

BREAKFAST	LUNCH	DINNER

SNACKS:

TOTAL CALORIES	GLASSES OF WATER	HOURS OF SLEEP

WEIGHT	BLOOD PRESSURE	BLOOD SUGAR

EXERCISE/ PHYSICAL ACTIVITY	SELF-CARE ACTIVITY

A friend loves at all times, and a brother is born for adversity.
(*Proverbs* 17:17)

DAY 130

SU MO TU WE TH FR SA

DATE: ____________________

How Do I Feel Today

☐ ☐ ☐ ☐

BREAKFAST	LUNCH	DINNER

SNACKS:

TOTAL CALORIES	GLASSES OF WATER	HOURS OF SLEEP

WEIGHT	BLOOD PRESSURE	BLOOD SUGAR

EXERCISE/ PHYSICAL ACTIVITY	SELF-CARE ACTIVITY

But God shows his love for me in that while I was still a sinner, Christ died for me.
(*Romans* 5:8)

DAY 131	SU MO TU WE TH FR SA DATE: ____________	How Do I Feel Today ☐ ☐ ☐ ☐

BREAKFAST	LUNCH	DINNER

SNACKS:

TOTAL CALORIES	**GLASSES OF WATER**	**HOURS OF SLEEP**

WEIGHT	**BLOOD PRESSURE**	**BLOOD SUGAR**

EXERCISE/ PHYSICAL ACTIVITY	**SELF-CARE ACTIVITY**

So now, faith, hope, and love abide, these three; but the greatest of these is love. (1 Corinthians 13:13)

DAY 132

SU MO TU WE TH FR SA

DATE: ____________________

How Do I Feel Today

☐ ☐ ☐ ☐

BREAKFAST	LUNCH	DINNER

SNACKS:

TOTAL CALORIES	GLASSES OF WATER	HOURS OF SLEEP

WEIGHT	BLOOD PRESSURE	BLOOD SUGAR

EXERCISE/ PHYSICAL ACTIVITY	SELF-CARE ACTIVITY

Love covers a multitude of sins. (1 Peter 4:8)

DAY 133	SU MO TU WE TH FR SA DATE: ______________	How Do I Feel Today ☐ ☐ ☐ ☐
BREAKFAST	LUNCH	DINNER
SNACKS:		
TOTAL CALORIES	GLASSES OF WATER	HOURS OF SLEEP
WEIGHT	BLOOD PRESSURE	BLOOD SUGAR
EXERCISE/ PHYSICAL ACTIVITY	SELF-CARE ACTIVITY	

Above all, put on love, which binds everything together in perfect harmony. (Colossians 3:14)

DAY 134

SU MO TU WE TH FR SA

DATE: ____________________

How Do I Feel Today

☐ ☐ ☐ ☐

BREAKFAST	LUNCH	DINNER

SNACKS:

TOTAL CALORIES	GLASSES OF WATER	HOURS OF SLEEP

WEIGHT	BLOOD PRESSURE	BLOOD SUGAR

EXERCISE/ PHYSICAL ACTIVITY	SELF-CARE ACTIVITY

"For God so loved the world, that he gave his only Son, that whoever believes in him should not perish but have eternal life. (John 3:16)

DAY 135

SU MO TU WE TH FR SA

DATE: ____________________

How Do I Feel Today

☐ ☐ ☐ ☐

BREAKFAST	LUNCH	DINNER

SNACKS:

TOTAL CALORIES	GLASSES OF WATER	HOURS OF SLEEP

WEIGHT	BLOOD PRESSURE	BLOOD SUGAR

EXERCISE/ PHYSICAL ACTIVITY	SELF-CARE ACTIVITY

All that I do will be done in love.
(1 Corinthians 16:14)

DAY 136

SU MO TU WE TH FR SA

DATE: ____________________

How Do I Feel Today

BREAKFAST	LUNCH	DINNER

SNACKS:

TOTAL CALORIES	**GLASSES OF WATER**	**HOURS OF SLEEP**

WEIGHT	**BLOOD PRESSURE**	**BLOOD SUGAR**

EXERCISE/ PHYSICAL ACTIVITY	**SELF-CARE ACTIVITY**

Love never ends. As for prophecies, they will pass away; as for tongues, they will cease; as for knowledge, it will pass away. (Hebrews 12: 2)

DAY 137

SU MO TU WE TH FR SA

DATE: ______________________

How Do I Feel Today

BREAKFAST	LUNCH	DINNER

SNACKS:

TOTAL CALORIES	GLASSES OF WATER	HOURS OF SLEEP

WEIGHT	BLOOD PRESSURE	BLOOD SUGAR

EXERCISE/ PHYSICAL ACTIVITY	SELF-CARE ACTIVITY

The Lord is faithful. He will establish me and guard me against the evil one. (2 Thessalonians 3:3)

DAY 138

SU MO TU WE TH FR SA

DATE: ____________________

How Do I Feel Today

☐ ☐ ☐ ☐

BREAKFAST	LUNCH	DINNER

SNACKS:

TOTAL CALORIES	GLASSES OF WATER	HOURS OF SLEEP

WEIGHT	BLOOD PRESSURE	BLOOD SUGAR

EXERCISE/ PHYSICAL ACTIVITY	SELF-CARE ACTIVITY

The Lord is my strength and my song; he has become my salvation.
(Psalm 118:14)

DAY 139

SU MO TU WE TH FR SA

DATE: ____________________

How Do I Feel Today

BREAKFAST	LUNCH	DINNER

SNACKS:

TOTAL CALORIES	GLASSES OF WATER	HOURS OF SLEEP

WEIGHT	BLOOD PRESSURE	BLOOD SUGAR

EXERCISE/ PHYSICAL ACTIVITY	SELF-CARE ACTIVITY

Even though I walk through the valley of the shadow of death, I will fear no evil,
for you are with me; your rod and your staff, they comfort me. (Psalm 23:4)

DAY 140

SU MO TU WE TH FR SA

DATE: ____________________

How Do I Feel Today

BREAKFAST	LUNCH	DINNER

SNACKS:

TOTAL CALORIES	**GLASSES OF WATER**	**HOURS OF SLEEP**

WEIGHT	**BLOOD PRESSURE**	**BLOOD SUGAR**

EXERCISE/ PHYSICAL ACTIVITY	**SELF-CARE ACTIVITY**

But you, Lord, are a shield around me, my glory, the One who lifts my head up high.
(*Psalm 3:3*)

DAY 141

SU MO TU WE TH FR SA

DATE: ____________________

How Do I Feel Today

☐ ☐ ☐ ☐

BREAKFAST	LUNCH	DINNER

SNACKS:

TOTAL CALORIES	**GLASSES OF WATER**	**HOURS OF SLEEP**

WEIGHT	**BLOOD PRESSURE**	**BLOOD SUGAR**

EXERCISE/ PHYSICAL ACTIVITY	**SELF-CARE ACTIVITY**

May the Lord give strength to his people! May the Lord bless his people with peace!
(Psalm 29:11)

DAY 142	SU MO TU WE TH FR SA	How Do I Feel Today
	DATE: ________________	☐ ☐ ☐ ☐

BREAKFAST	LUNCH	DINNER

SNACKS:

TOTAL CALORIES	GLASSES OF WATER	HOURS OF SLEEP

WEIGHT	BLOOD PRESSURE	BLOOD SUGAR

EXERCISE/ PHYSICAL ACTIVITY	SELF-CARE ACTIVITY

The Sovereign Lord gives me strength. He makes me sure-footed as a deer and keeps me safe on the mountains. (Habakkuk 3:19)

DAY 143	SU MO TU WE TH FR SA DATE: ______________	How Do I Feel Today ☐ ☐ ☐ ☐

BREAKFAST	LUNCH	DINNER

SNACKS:

TOTAL CALORIES	GLASSES OF WATER	HOURS OF SLEEP

WEIGHT	BLOOD PRESSURE	BLOOD SUGAR

EXERCISE/ PHYSICAL ACTIVITY	SELF-CARE ACTIVITY

God is my refuge and strength, a very present help in trouble.
(*Psalm* 46:1)

DAY 144	SU MO TU WE TH FR SA DATE: ______________	How Do I Feel Today

BREAKFAST	LUNCH	DINNER

SNACKS:

TOTAL CALORIES	GLASSES OF WATER	HOURS OF SLEEP

WEIGHT	BLOOD PRESSURE	BLOOD SUGAR

EXERCISE/ PHYSICAL ACTIVITY	SELF-CARE ACTIVITY

This day is holy to the Lord. I will not be grieved, for the joy of the Lord is my strength.
(Nehemiah 8:10)

DAY 145

SU MO TU WE TH FR SA

DATE: ____________________

How Do I Feel Today

☐ ☐ ☐ ☐

BREAKFAST	LUNCH	DINNER

SNACKS:

TOTAL CALORIES	**GLASSES OF WATER**	**HOURS OF SLEEP**

WEIGHT	**BLOOD PRESSURE**	**BLOOD SUGAR**

EXERCISE/ PHYSICAL ACTIVITY	**SELF-CARE ACTIVITY**

His grace is sufficient for me, for His power is made perfect in weakness.
(2 Corinthians 12:9)

DAY 146	SU MO TU WE TH FR SA DATE: ______	How Do I Feel Today ☐ ☐ ☐ ☐
BREAKFAST	LUNCH	DINNER

SNACKS:

TOTAL CALORIES	GLASSES OF WATER	HOURS OF SLEEP

WEIGHT	BLOOD PRESSURE	BLOOD SUGAR

EXERCISE/ PHYSICAL ACTIVITY	SELF-CARE ACTIVITY

I will boast all the more gladly of my weaknesses, so that the power of Christ may rest upon me.
(2 Corinthians 12:9)

DAY 147

SU MO TU WE TH FR SA

DATE: ____________________

How Do I Feel Today

BREAKFAST	LUNCH	DINNER

SNACKS:

TOTAL CALORIES	GLASSES OF WATER	HOURS OF SLEEP

WEIGHT	BLOOD PRESSURE	BLOOD SUGAR

EXERCISE/ PHYSICAL ACTIVITY	SELF-CARE ACTIVITY

My flesh and my heart may fail, but God is the strength of my heart and my portion forever.
(*Psalm 73:26*)

DAY 148	SU MO TU WE TH FR SA DATE: ____________	How Do I Feel Today ☐ ☐ ☐ ☐
BREAKFAST	LUNCH	DINNER

SNACKS:

TOTAL CALORIES	GLASSES OF WATER	HOURS OF SLEEP

WEIGHT	BLOOD PRESSURE	BLOOD SUGAR

EXERCISE/ PHYSICAL ACTIVITY	SELF-CARE ACTIVITY

I will be strong and courageous, because my hope is in the Lord!
(Psalm 31:24)

DAY 149

SU MO TU WE TH FR SA

DATE: ______________

How Do I Feel Today

BREAKFAST	LUNCH	DINNER

SNACKS:

TOTAL CALORIES	GLASSES OF WATER	HOURS OF SLEEP

WEIGHT	BLOOD PRESSURE	BLOOD SUGAR

EXERCISE/ PHYSICAL ACTIVITY	SELF-CARE ACTIVITY

The Lord is my light and my salvation; whom shall I fear? The Lord is the strength of my life; of whom shall I be afraid? (Psalm 27:1)

DAY 150	SU MO TU WE TH FR SA DATE: ______________	How Do I Feel Today ☐ ☐ ☐ ☐
BREAKFAST	LUNCH	DINNER

SNACKS:

TOTAL CALORIES	GLASSES OF WATER	HOURS OF SLEEP

WEIGHT	BLOOD PRESSURE	BLOOD SUGAR

EXERCISE/ PHYSICAL ACTIVITY	SELF-CARE ACTIVITY

He gives strength to the weary and increases the power of the weak.
(Isaiah 40:29)

DAY 151	SU MO TU WE TH FR SA DATE: ____________	How Do I Feel Today ☐ ☐ ☐ ☐

BREAKFAST	LUNCH	DINNER

SNACKS:

TOTAL CALORIES	GLASSES OF WATER	HOURS OF SLEEP

WEIGHT	BLOOD PRESSURE	BLOOD SUGAR

EXERCISE/ PHYSICAL ACTIVITY	SELF-CARE ACTIVITY

I will trust, and will not be afraid; for the Lord God is my strength and my song, and he has become my salvation. (Isaiah 12:2)

DAY 152	SU MO TU WE TH FR SA DATE: ____________	How Do I Feel Today ☐ ☐ ☐ ☐

BREAKFAST	LUNCH	DINNER

SNACKS:

TOTAL CALORIES	GLASSES OF WATER	HOURS OF SLEEP

WEIGHT	BLOOD PRESSURE	BLOOD SUGAR

EXERCISE/ PHYSICAL ACTIVITY	SELF-CARE ACTIVITY

Surely your goodness and love will follow me all the days of my life,
and I will dwell in the house of the Lord for ever. (Psalm 23:6)

DAY 153

SU MO TU WE TH FR SA

DATE: ____________________

How Do I Feel Today

☐ ☐ ☐ ☐

BREAKFAST	LUNCH	DINNER

SNACKS:

TOTAL CALORIES	GLASSES OF WATER	HOURS OF SLEEP

WEIGHT	BLOOD PRESSURE	BLOOD SUGAR

EXERCISE/ PHYSICAL ACTIVITY	SELF-CARE ACTIVITY

For the Lord my God is he who goes with me to fight for me against the enemy, to give me the victory. (Deuteronomy 20:4)

DAY 154

SU MO TU WE TH FR SA

DATE: ____________________

How Do I Feel Today

BREAKFAST	LUNCH	DINNER

SNACKS:

TOTAL CALORIES	GLASSES OF WATER	HOURS OF SLEEP

WEIGHT	BLOOD PRESSURE	BLOOD SUGAR

EXERCISE/ PHYSICAL ACTIVITY	SELF-CARE ACTIVITY

I am strong in the Lord and in His mighty power.
(Ephesians 6:10)

DAY 155

SU MO TU WE TH FR SA

DATE: ___________________

How Do I Feel Today

☐ ☐ ☐ ☐

BREAKFAST	LUNCH	DINNER

SNACKS:

TOTAL CALORIES	GLASSES OF WATER	HOURS OF SLEEP

WEIGHT	BLOOD PRESSURE	BLOOD SUGAR

EXERCISE/ PHYSICAL ACTIVITY	SELF-CARE ACTIVITY

Those who wait for the Lord shall renew their strength; they shall mount up with wings like eagles; They shall run and not be weary; they shall walk and not faint. (Isaiah 40:31)

DAY 156

SU MO TU WE TH FR SA

DATE: ______________

How Do I Feel Today

☐ ☐ ☐ ☐

BREAKFAST	LUNCH	DINNER

SNACKS:

TOTAL CALORIES	GLASSES OF WATER	HOURS OF SLEEP

WEIGHT	BLOOD PRESSURE	BLOOD SUGAR

EXERCISE/ PHYSICAL ACTIVITY	SELF-CARE ACTIVITY

I will be strong and courageous. I will not fear, for the Lord my God goes with me. He will never leave me or forsake me. (Deuteronomy 31:6)

DAY 157	SU MO TU WE TH FR SA DATE: ____________	How Do I Feel Today ☐ ☐ ☐ ☐
BREAKFAST	LUNCH	DINNER

SNACKS:

TOTAL CALORIES	GLASSES OF WATER	HOURS OF SLEEP

WEIGHT	BLOOD PRESSURE	BLOOD SUGAR

EXERCISE/ PHYSICAL ACTIVITY	SELF-CARE ACTIVITY

I will not fear, for the Lord is with me; I will not be dismayed, for He is my God; He will strengthen me and help me, he will uphold me with His righteous right hand. (Isaiah 41:10)

DAY 158

SU MO TU WE TH FR SA

DATE: ____________________

How Do I Feel Today

☐ ☐ ☐ ☐

BREAKFAST	LUNCH	DINNER

SNACKS:

TOTAL CALORIES	GLASSES OF WATER	HOURS OF SLEEP

WEIGHT	BLOOD PRESSURE	BLOOD SUGAR

EXERCISE/ PHYSICAL ACTIVITY	SELF-CARE ACTIVITY

I can do all things through Christ who strengthens me.
(Philippians 4:13)

DAY 159

SU MO TU WE TH FR SA

DATE: ____________________

How Do I Feel Today

BREAKFAST	LUNCH	DINNER

SNACKS:

TOTAL CALORIES	GLASSES OF WATER	HOURS OF SLEEP

WEIGHT	BLOOD PRESSURE	BLOOD SUGAR

EXERCISE/ PHYSICAL ACTIVITY	SELF-CARE ACTIVITY

Since, I have been raised up with Christ, I will set my heart on things above, where Christ is, seated at the right hand of God. (Colossians 3:1)

DAY 160	SU MO TU WE TH FR SA DATE: ______________	How Do I Feel Today

BREAKFAST	LUNCH	DINNER

SNACKS:

TOTAL CALORIES	GLASSES OF WATER	HOURS OF SLEEP

WEIGHT	BLOOD PRESSURE	BLOOD SUGAR

EXERCISE/ PHYSICAL ACTIVITY	SELF-CARE ACTIVITY

May the eyes of my understanding be enlightened; so that I may know what is the hope of His calling, and what are the riches of the glory of His inheritance in the saints. (Ephesians 1:18)

DAY 161	SU MO TU WE TH FR SA DATE: ________________	How Do I Feel Today ☐ ☐ ☐ ☐

BREAKFAST	LUNCH	DINNER

SNACKS:

TOTAL CALORIES	GLASSES OF WATER	HOURS OF SLEEP

WEIGHT	BLOOD PRESSURE	BLOOD SUGAR

EXERCISE/ PHYSICAL ACTIVITY	SELF-CARE ACTIVITY

I will not focus on the things which are seen, but on the things which are not seen. For the things which are seen are temporary, but the things which are not seen are eternal. (2 Corinthians 4:17-18)

DAY 162

SU MO TU WE TH FR SA

DATE: ____________________

How Do I Feel Today

BREAKFAST	LUNCH	DINNER

SNACKS:

TOTAL CALORIES	GLASSES OF WATER	HOURS OF SLEEP

WEIGHT	BLOOD PRESSURE	BLOOD SUGAR

EXERCISE/ PHYSICAL ACTIVITY	SELF-CARE ACTIVITY

He who sows to the Spirit will of the Spirit reap everlasting life. (Galatians 6:8)

DAY 163

SU MO TU WE TH FR SA

DATE: ____________________

How Do I Feel Today

☐ ☐ ☐ ☐

BREAKFAST	LUNCH	DINNER

SNACKS:

TOTAL CALORIES	GLASSES OF WATER	HOURS OF SLEEP

WEIGHT	BLOOD PRESSURE	BLOOD SUGAR

EXERCISE/ PHYSICAL ACTIVITY	SELF-CARE ACTIVITY

I am a child of God; and it has not yet been revealed what I will be, but I know that when He is revealed, I will be like Him, for I will see Him as He is. (1 John 3:2)

DAY 164	SU MO TU WE TH FR SA DATE: ________________	How Do I Feel Today ☐ ☐ ☐ ☐

BREAKFAST	LUNCH	DINNER

SNACKS:

TOTAL CALORIES	GLASSES OF WATER	HOURS OF SLEEP

WEIGHT	BLOOD PRESSURE	BLOOD SUGAR

EXERCISE/ PHYSICAL ACTIVITY	SELF-CARE ACTIVITY

My hope is in Christ.
(Psalm 39:7)

DAY 165	SU MO TU WE TH FR SA DATE: ______________	How Do I Feel Today ☐ ☐ ☐ ☐

BREAKFAST	LUNCH	DINNER

SNACKS:

TOTAL CALORIES	GLASSES OF WATER	HOURS OF SLEEP

WEIGHT	BLOOD PRESSURE	BLOOD SUGAR

EXERCISE/ PHYSICAL ACTIVITY	SELF-CARE ACTIVITY

For God knew his people in advance, and he chose them to become like his Son, so that his Son would be the firstborn among many brothers and sisters. (Romans 8:29)

DAY 166

SU MO TU WE TH FR SA

DATE: ____________________

How Do I Feel Today

☐ ☐ ☐ ☐

BREAKFAST	LUNCH	DINNER

SNACKS:

TOTAL CALORIES	GLASSES OF WATER	HOURS OF SLEEP

WEIGHT	BLOOD PRESSURE	BLOOD SUGAR

EXERCISE/ PHYSICAL ACTIVITY	SELF-CARE ACTIVITY

For his Spirit joins with our spirit to affirm that we are God's children, since we are His children, we are his heirs, and joint heirs with Christ Jesus. (Romans 8:16-17)

DAY 167

SU MO TU WE TH FR SA

DATE: ____________________

How Do I Feel Today

BREAKFAST	LUNCH	DINNER

SNACKS:

TOTAL CALORIES	**GLASSES OF WATER**	**HOURS OF SLEEP**

WEIGHT	**BLOOD PRESSURE**	**BLOOD SUGAR**

EXERCISE/ PHYSICAL ACTIVITY	**SELF-CARE ACTIVITY**

Christ is living in me, giving me the hope of glory. (Colossians 1:27)

DAY 168

SU MO TU WE TH FR SA

DATE: ____________

How Do I Feel Today

☐ ☐ ☐ ☐

BREAKFAST	LUNCH	DINNER

SNACKS:

TOTAL CALORIES	GLASSES OF WATER	HOURS OF SLEEP

WEIGHT	BLOOD PRESSURE	BLOOD SUGAR

EXERCISE/ PHYSICAL ACTIVITY	SELF-CARE ACTIVITY

He who has begun a good work in me will complete it until the day of Jesus Christ.
(Philippians 1:6)

DAY 169	SU MO TU WE TH FR SA DATE: ____________	How Do I Feel Today ☐ ☐ ☐ ☐

BREAKFAST	LUNCH	DINNER

SNACKS:

TOTAL CALORIES	GLASSES OF WATER	HOURS OF SLEEP

WEIGHT	BLOOD PRESSURE	BLOOD SUGAR

EXERCISE/ PHYSICAL ACTIVITY	SELF-CARE ACTIVITY

I consider that the sufferings of this present time are not worthy to be compared with the glory, which shall be revealed in us. (Romans 8:18)

DAY 170	SU MO TU WE TH FR SA DATE: ______________	How Do I Feel Today ☐ ☐ ☐ ☐
BREAKFAST	LUNCH	DINNER

SNACKS:

TOTAL CALORIES	GLASSES OF WATER	HOURS OF SLEEP

WEIGHT	BLOOD PRESSURE	BLOOD SUGAR

EXERCISE/ PHYSICAL ACTIVITY	SELF-CARE ACTIVITY

For I know the thoughts that I think towards you, says the Lord,
thoughts of peace and not of evil, to give you a bright hope and an awesome future. (Jeremiah 29:11)

DAY 171

SU MO TU WE TH FR SA

DATE: ____________

How Do I Feel Today

☐ ☐ ☐ ☐

BREAKFAST	LUNCH	DINNER

SNACKS:

TOTAL CALORIES	GLASSES OF WATER	HOURS OF SLEEP

WEIGHT	BLOOD PRESSURE	BLOOD SUGAR

EXERCISE/ PHYSICAL ACTIVITY	SELF-CARE ACTIVITY

Fear not, for I have redeemed you; I have called you by your name; you are Mine, says the Lord.
(Isaiah 43:1)

DAY 172	SU MO TU WE TH FR SA DATE: ____________	How Do I Feel Today ☐ ☐ ☐ ☐

BREAKFAST	LUNCH	DINNER

SNACKS:

TOTAL CALORIES	GLASSES OF WATER	HOURS OF SLEEP

WEIGHT	BLOOD PRESSURE	BLOOD SUGAR

EXERCISE/ PHYSICAL ACTIVITY	SELF-CARE ACTIVITY

When I go through deep waters, He will be with me.
When I go through rivers of difficulty, I will not drown. (Isaiah 43:2)

DAY 173

SU MO TU WE TH FR SA

DATE: ______________________

How Do I Feel Today

BREAKFAST	LUNCH	DINNER

SNACKS:

TOTAL CALORIES	GLASSES OF WATER	HOURS OF SLEEP

WEIGHT	BLOOD PRESSURE	BLOOD SUGAR

EXERCISE/ PHYSICAL ACTIVITY	SELF-CARE ACTIVITY

When I walk through the fire of oppression, I will not be burned up;
the flames will not consume me. (Isaiah 43:2)

DAY 174

SU MO TU WE TH FR SA

DATE: ___________________

How Do I Feel Today

☐ ☐ ☐ ☐

BREAKFAST	LUNCH	DINNER

SNACKS:

TOTAL CALORIES	GLASSES OF WATER	HOURS OF SLEEP

WEIGHT	BLOOD PRESSURE	BLOOD SUGAR

EXERCISE/ PHYSICAL ACTIVITY	SELF-CARE ACTIVITY

The faithful love of the Lord never ends! His mercies never cease. They are new every morning. Great is His faithfulness. (Lamentations 3:22)

DAY 175

SU MO TU WE TH FR SA

DATE: ____________________

How Do I Feel Today

☐ ☐ ☐ ☐

BREAKFAST	LUNCH	DINNER

SNACKS:

TOTAL CALORIES	**GLASSES OF WATER**	**HOURS OF SLEEP**

WEIGHT	**BLOOD PRESSURE**	**BLOOD SUGAR**

EXERCISE/ PHYSICAL ACTIVITY	**SELF-CARE ACTIVITY**

Blessed is the one who trusts in the Lord, whose confidence is in him. (Jeremiah 17:7)

DAY 176

SU MO TU WE TH FR SA

DATE: ____________________

How Do I Feel Today

☐ ☐ ☐ ☐

BREAKFAST	LUNCH	DINNER

SNACKS:

TOTAL CALORIES	**GLASSES OF WATER**	**HOURS OF SLEEP**

WEIGHT	**BLOOD PRESSURE**	**BLOOD SUGAR**

EXERCISE/ PHYSICAL ACTIVITY	**SELF-CARE ACTIVITY**

If we hope for what we do not see, we eagerly wait for it with perseverance.
(Romans 8:25)

DAY 177

SU MO TU WE TH FR SA

DATE: ____________

How Do I Feel Today

☐ ☐ ☐ ☐

BREAKFAST	LUNCH	DINNER

SNACKS:

TOTAL CALORIES	**GLASSES OF WATER**	**HOURS OF SLEEP**

WEIGHT	**BLOOD PRESSURE**	**BLOOD SUGAR**

EXERCISE/ PHYSICAL ACTIVITY	**SELF-CARE ACTIVITY**

Hope does not disappoint, because the love of God has been poured out in our hearts by the Holy Spirit who was given to us. (Romans 5:5)

DAY 178	SU MO TU WE TH FR SA DATE: ______________	How Do I Feel Today ☐ ☐ ☐ ☐

BREAKFAST	LUNCH	DINNER

SNACKS:

TOTAL CALORIES	GLASSES OF WATER	HOURS OF SLEEP

WEIGHT	BLOOD PRESSURE	BLOOD SUGAR

EXERCISE/ PHYSICAL ACTIVITY	SELF-CARE ACTIVITY

Jesus is able, once and forever, to save those who come to God through him. He lives forever to intercede with God on their behalf. (Hebrews 7:25)

DAY 179

SU MO TU WE TH FR SA

DATE: ____________

How Do I Feel Today

BREAKFAST	LUNCH	DINNER

SNACKS:

TOTAL CALORIES	GLASSES OF WATER	HOURS OF SLEEP

WEIGHT	BLOOD PRESSURE	BLOOD SUGAR

EXERCISE/ PHYSICAL ACTIVITY	SELF-CARE ACTIVITY

The Lord is my light and my salvation; whom shall I fear?
The Lord is the strength of my life; of whom shall I be afraid? (Psalm 27:1)

DAY 180

SU MO TU WE TH FR SA

DATE: ____________________

How Do I Feel Today

BREAKFAST	LUNCH	DINNER

SNACKS:

TOTAL CALORIES	GLASSES OF WATER	HOURS OF SLEEP

WEIGHT	BLOOD PRESSURE	BLOOD SUGAR

EXERCISE/ PHYSICAL ACTIVITY	SELF-CARE ACTIVITY

The Lord my God is with me, the Mighty Warrior who saves. He takes great delight in me.
(Zephaniah 3:17)

DAY 181

SU MO TU WE TH FR SA

DATE: ____________________

How Do I Feel Today

☐ ☐ ☐ ☐

BREAKFAST	LUNCH	DINNER

SNACKS:

TOTAL CALORIES	GLASSES OF WATER	HOURS OF SLEEP

WEIGHT	BLOOD PRESSURE	BLOOD SUGAR

EXERCISE/ PHYSICAL ACTIVITY	SELF-CARE ACTIVITY

Be strong and courageous. Do not fear or be in dread of them, for it is the Lord your God who goes with you. He will not leave you or forsake you. (Lamentations 3:22-23)

DAY 182	SU MO TU WE TH FR SA DATE: ____________	How Do I Feel Today ☐ ☐ ☐ ☐
BREAKFAST	LUNCH	DINNER

SNACKS:

TOTAL CALORIES	GLASSES OF WATER	HOURS OF SLEEP

WEIGHT	BLOOD PRESSURE	BLOOD SUGAR

EXERCISE/ PHYSICAL ACTIVITY	SELF-CARE ACTIVITY

Oh, taste and see that the Lord is good! Blessed is the man who takes refuge in him! (Psalm 34:8)

DAY 183

SU MO TU WE TH FR SA

DATE: ____________

How Do I Feel Today

☐ ☐ ☐ ☐

BREAKFAST	LUNCH	DINNER

SNACKS:

TOTAL CALORIES	**GLASSES OF WATER**	**HOURS OF SLEEP**

WEIGHT	**BLOOD PRESSURE**	**BLOOD SUGAR**

EXERCISE/ PHYSICAL ACTIVITY	**SELF-CARE ACTIVITY**

Be steadfast, immovable, always abounding in the work of the Lord, knowing that your labor, in the Lord, will not be in vain. (1 Corinthians 15:58)

DAY 184

SU MO TU WE TH FR SA

DATE: ____________

How Do I Feel Today

BREAKFAST	LUNCH	DINNER

SNACKS:

TOTAL CALORIES	GLASSES OF WATER	HOURS OF SLEEP

WEIGHT	BLOOD PRESSURE	BLOOD SUGAR

EXERCISE/ PHYSICAL ACTIVITY	SELF-CARE ACTIVITY

Fear not, for I am with you; be not dismayed, for I am your God; I will strengthen you, I will help you, I will uphold you with my righteous right hand. (Isaiah 41:10)

DAY 185

SU MO TU WE TH FR SA

DATE: ____________________

How Do I Feel Today

BREAKFAST	LUNCH	DINNER

SNACKS:

TOTAL CALORIES	GLASSES OF WATER	HOURS OF SLEEP

WEIGHT	BLOOD PRESSURE	BLOOD SUGAR

EXERCISE/ PHYSICAL ACTIVITY	SELF-CARE ACTIVITY

The Lord is my shepherd; I shall not want.
(Psalm 23:1)

DAY 186

SU MO TU WE TH FR SA

DATE: ____________________

How Do I Feel Today

BREAKFAST	LUNCH	DINNER

SNACKS:

TOTAL CALORIES	**GLASSES OF WATER**	**HOURS OF SLEEP**

WEIGHT	**BLOOD PRESSURE**	**BLOOD SUGAR**

EXERCISE/ PHYSICAL ACTIVITY	**SELF-CARE ACTIVITY**

God is within me, I will not fall; From the very break of day, God will protect me.
(Psalm 46:5)

DAY 187

SU MO TU WE TH FR SA

DATE: ____________________

How Do I Feel Today

BREAKFAST	LUNCH	DINNER

SNACKS:

TOTAL CALORIES	GLASSES OF WATER	HOURS OF SLEEP

WEIGHT	BLOOD PRESSURE	BLOOD SUGAR

EXERCISE/ PHYSICAL ACTIVITY	SELF-CARE ACTIVITY

Anyone who belongs to Christ has become a new person. The old life is gone; a new life has begun!
(2 Corinthians 5:17)

DAY 188

SU MO TU WE TH FR SA

DATE: ____________________

How Do I Feel Today

BREAKFAST	LUNCH	DINNER

SNACKS:

TOTAL CALORIES	**GLASSES OF WATER**	**HOURS OF SLEEP**

WEIGHT	**BLOOD PRESSURE**	**BLOOD SUGAR**

EXERCISE/ PHYSICAL ACTIVITY	**SELF-CARE ACTIVITY**

I sought the Lord, and he answered me; he delivered me from all my fears.
Those who look to him are radiant; their faces are never covered with shame. (Psalm 34:4-5)

DAY 189	SU MO TU WE TH FR SA DATE: ___________	How Do I Feel Today ☐ ☐ ☐ ☐

BREAKFAST	LUNCH	DINNER

SNACKS:

TOTAL CALORIES	GLASSES OF WATER	HOURS OF SLEEP

WEIGHT	BLOOD PRESSURE	BLOOD SUGAR

EXERCISE/ PHYSICAL ACTIVITY	SELF-CARE ACTIVITY

I took my troubles to the Lord; I cried out to him, and he answered my prayer.
(*Psalm* 120:1)

DAY 190	SU MO TU WE TH FR SA DATE: ______________	How Do I Feel Today ☐ ☐ ☐ ☐
BREAKFAST	LUNCH	DINNER

SNACKS:

TOTAL CALORIES	GLASSES OF WATER	HOURS OF SLEEP

WEIGHT	BLOOD PRESSURE	BLOOD SUGAR

EXERCISE/ PHYSICAL ACTIVITY	SELF-CARE ACTIVITY

I will lay aside every weight, and the sin which so easily beset me, and I will run with patience the race that is set before me. (Hebrews 12:1)

The End Point

Current Stats

- Blood Pressure: ______________________
- Blood Sugar: ______________________
- Cholesterol: ______________________
- Weight: ______________________
- Thigh: ______________________
- Waist: ______________________
- Hips: ______________________
- BMI: ______________________

Overall Feelings *Toward:*

where you are at this point in your journey compared to where you were when you started and where you had expected to be at this point.

Reflections

I have fought a good fight, I have finished my course, I have kept the faith.
(2 Timothy 4:7)

Reflect on the goals that you have made at the beginning of your journey

Which goals did you accomplish?
Which goals did you not accomplish?
Explain Below...

Diet

Exercise

Weight Loss

Selfcare

Blood pressure, blood sugar, cholesterol levels etc.

Reflections on Goals

But none of these things move me, neither count I *my life dear unto myself, so that* I *might finish my course with joy, to testify of the gospel of the grace of* God. (Acts 20:24)

Now *that you have come to the end of this phase of your health, wellness and self-care journey, how has your perspective (concerning diet, exercise, weight loss, selfcare etc.) been affected by your experiences over the past 6 months?*

Reflections

The patient in spirit is better than the proud in spirit. (Ecclesiastes 7:8)

What are your goals for the next phase of your health, wellness & selfcare journey?

Diet, exercise, weight loss, selfcare
Blood sugar, blood pressure & cholesterol levels etc.

Made in the USA
Las Vegas, NV
25 April 2025

21307612R00115